Frederick Sydney Wilson

Australian Songs and Poems

Frederick Sydney Wilson

Australian Songs and Poems

ISBN/EAN: 9783337007072

Printed in Europe, USA, Canada, Australia, Japan

Cover: Foto ©Thomas Meinert / pixelio.de

More available books at **www.hansebooks.com**

Australian

Songs and Poems

By

Frederick Sydney Wilson.

Sydney:
Gibbs, Shallard, & Co., Printers & Publishers,
123 Pitt Street, next Union Bank.

1870.

TO

THE PEOPLE OF AUSTRALIA,

THIS

COLLECTION OF FIRST EFFORTS

IS DEDICATED.

BY

AN AUSTRALIAN.

Sydney,

March, 1870.

Contents.

	PAGE.
CHRISTMAS POEMS:—	
Five Thousand Leagues Away	11
The Old Year and the New	17
Five Years Ago	21
LAYS OF ILLAWARRA :—	
Illawarra	26
Coming Events	32
Jamberoo	36
The Beach of Wollongong	41
Terrara	47
Gerringong	50
POEMS OF THE AUSTRALIAN BUSH :—	
Lost in the Bush	65
The Mountain Moss Spring	69

CONTENTS.

POEMS OF THE AUSTRALIAN BUSH—*continued*:—

	PAGE.
WAITING FOR THE MAIL	73
ARAKOON	77
SUNSET IN THE FOREST	84
SUCH IS THE WAY OF THE WORLD	88

SEA-SIDE LYRICS:—

FLOATING AWAY	95
ST. VALENTINE'S EVE	98
UNDER THE CLIFFS	103
VOICES FROM THE SEA	109
FOOTPRINTS IN THE SAND	114
BONDI	117

MISCELLANEOUS POEMS:—

OLD MEMORIES	125
DROWNED	130
THE STRANDED BOAT	134
TWO AUSTRALIAN PICTURES	138
SHADOWS ON THE WALL	147

CONTENTS.

	PAGE.
MISCELLANEOUS POEMS—*continued* :—	
Advance Australia	151
God Bless Our Sailor Prince	156
Coming Down the River	161
SONGS AND BALLADS :—	
The Australian Stockman's Song	167
There's No Such Word as Fail	170
The Cricket on the Hearth	173
Her Memory Lingers Yet	176
Think of Me!	179
Only of Thee, Love!	181
Stars of Heaven	184
Beside the Garden Gate	186
FRAGMENTS FROM "KIANDRA" :—	
Ninety-five Days Out	191
Morning in the Australian Alps	198

Christmas Poems.

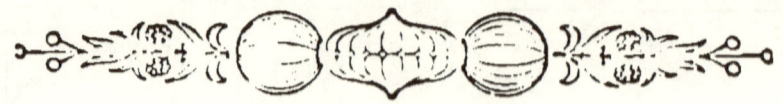

Five Thousand Leagues Away.

A CHRISTMAS LYRIC.

Like the low sweet voice of a wandering tide
   that returns to its own loved shore,
The waves of Memory flood my heart with a
   dream of the days of yore ;
My brain is filled with a pleasant song—a
   ballad of bygone times—
Again I hear the old church bells ringing
   their Christmas chimes !
Ringing the chimes, while the circling rooks
   are floating about the spires,
And the outside snow is all aglow with the
   gleam of cottage fires—

My lips are moved with a thankful
prayer—
" God's blessing on the day
That links my heart to the absent
ones
Five thousand leagues away!"

Yes!—this is the happy Christmas-time; and
yet how strange it seems!
The crimson flush on the flowering brush—
the flame on the splendid streams!
The sun's bold glance—the mirage-dance of
the bright Australian noon
As the warm-breath'd breeze just stirs the
trees that girdle the broad lagoon.
Still as I gaze on the blooms that fringe the
wild creek's sunny flow,

I think of faces far away where the fields are
    white with snow!
        And wonder and weep—" Will their
            memories keep,
      'Mid the mirth of this gladsome
        day,
    A sacred place for an absent face
      Five thousand leagues away!"

Again I see the old elm-tree, with its branches
    bleak and bare—
And the rustic seat where lovers meet—yes!
    lovers and seat are there!
And I fancy I know that arch bright smile—
    the turn of the glittering curl
That hangs (like the spray of a fruitful vine)
    on the neck of a lovely girl!

And the sterner face, above her bent, is lit with a softer light
As her voice falls low like a wavelet's song when sunset fades to night,
    And they list to the merry Christmas chimes
    And laugh!—ah! well-a-day!
    Does *she* ever think of a changeless face
    Five thousand leagues away!

The snow may rest in last year's nest that hangs on the hazel copse—
But the birds will flit through the boughs, and sit again in the rocking tops,
Tho' the cottage eaves are lone, and miss the flash of a welcome wing,

We know the swallows will come again with
the sunshine and the spring—
And so, returned, an old old love in each
true bosom swells,
When the sad-sweet rhyme of an ancient time
chimes in with the Christmas bells.
 Ah ! *then* their memories turn to me,
  And " God's blessing," still I pray,
 " On the eyes that dim when they
  think of him
   Five thousand leagues away."

I know Life's time of golden prime—the
beautiful time of yore—
Has faded away, like a fallen star that will
shine in heaven no more !
And I sometimes yearn to backward turn my
steps, and a day re-live,

That my lips might sound the happy laugh
that only a child can give!
But ah!—'tis vain, we can ne'er regain our
Childhood's sand of gold—
'Tis well, as our bodies fade and fail, if our
spirits grow not old!
    That heart to heart in love may start
      With the bells of each Christmas
day,
    " Lord, keep our memories green "
      for those
      Five thousand leagues away!

The Old Year and the New.

Lonely and gloomily bells toll forth
  The dirge of the parting year!
Dying away with a wearisome moan—
Like the low, sad wail of a sorrowful crone—
They clang—clang—clang—with a deadened
    tone,
  Drearily on the ear!
Floating, and floating, away they roll,
Now faint in the distance we hear them toll—
  Now in the clear
  Calm night draw near
  And multitudes follow a funeral bier!—
The heart-sick and weary, the stricken and
    old—

Youth, in its innocence, careless and bold;
The poor with his hunger—the rich with his gold—
All gathered together—the young and the old—
  To bury the poor Old Year!
Bury him deep—
Sound be his sleep!
Tears for the past on his coffin-lid weep;
And throw in the grave, with his care wrinkled crust,
The grudges we bore 'gainst the honest and just—
The festering hate, and the passionate lust—
The deep love of gold—let them rotten and rust!—
Ashes to ashes, and dust to dust.
  Farewell! thou poor Old Year.

Cheerily—merrily—bells ring out
   A peal to the coming year!
Joyously—heartily!—Hark how they chime!
Telling of Peace in Australia's fair clime—
And of happiness borne on the wings of Old
    Time,
   To banish each sorrowful tear!
Their silvery melody speaks of a life
Gladden'd with goodness, unclouded by strife;
   While, bright and clear,
   Visions appear,
Picturing all that Affection holds dear!
A loved one to love, when Adversity lours,
Forming a rainbow to brighten its showers,
And strewing our paths with unwithering
    flowers—
      This be our glad New Year.
  May virtues unfold

As our years grow old,
And the dross and defilement be purged from our gold!
May our bosoms grow heavy with sympathy's sigh
When we look on the grief of a tear-moisten'd eye—
And still, as the Night of our life hurries by,
And the Morning that never shall end draws nigh—
May this be our greeting—this be our cry :—
    Welcome! thou Happy New Year.

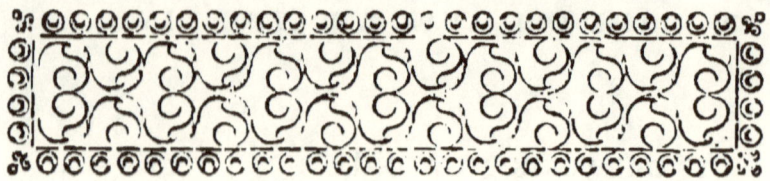

Five Years Ago.

A CHRISTMAS REVERIE.

O, SWEETLY falls the summershine on rocky cleft and ledge—
Where the fig-tree's bare and twisted roots creep to the river's edge;
And the sparkles shoot from the shelly beach, and over the ripples play,
While the pleasant chime of the Christmas bells comes stealing up the bay!
    The mossy pools look calmly up,
        And bask in the sun's rich glow—
    But they miss the light of a welcome face
        They knew five years ago!

Beauty and Youth are resting now, beneath
    the same old tree,
And watch the bubbles that float along—to
    die in a stormy sea !—
The eyes are bright that our glances meet,
    and their laugh is the laugh of yore,
But it brings a dream of a quiet face that will
    greet us never more !
      It speaks of tones that told of love
        In whispers sweet and low ;
      As we sat by the river's grassy brink
        Five changeful years ago !

The wattle showers its golden flowers to fall
    in the rushing tide,
As when in the youth of Love and Truth we
    stood by the water-side ;

And the spectral ships, that we saw depart,
    come back from the rolling main—
But oh! for the sound of a gentle voice that
    will never return again!
        The wattle may shake its golden curls,
            The ripples may meet and flow—
        But the song they sing is a sad refrain
            Of " Five long years ago!"

We mourn:—and yet should we regret the
    loss of a smiling face,
When true and faithful hearts remain to fill
    the vacant place?
If thoughts recall an absent voice that *once*
    was true and kind,
O let our thoughts still closer cling to the
    loved ones left behind!

For vainly fondest hopes may yearn—
And vainly tear-drops flow
For one who sank in the Christmas time,
Five weary years ago!

While friendly hands grasp friendly hands, and the summer of life is ours,—
'Tis then we may choke their way with thorns, or scatter their path with flowers!
'Tis ours to calm the fluttering fear, and the bosom's burning pain,
Till fainting Love—like a weary dove—returns to the heart again!
Yes! some are left to live for still,
Tho' we speak in whispers low
Of the flower that bloom'd in the Christmas time
Five changeful years ago!

Lays of Illawarra.

Illawarra.

Illawarra!—Home of beauty!—Land of forest, flower, and fern!
Let me loiter where the headlands in the blaze of Summer burn—
Where the shifting shafts of sunshine bar with gold the sounding shore,
And the sea-fowl's scream is mated with the bursting billow's roar—
Where the crags are grey and splinter'd—worn of wind, and reft of rain—
Let me all the past remember—let me be a boy again;

Freed from clanking chains of Commerce, and the click of clerkly pen,
I would revel in the music born of wild-wood, sea, and glen.

Here a mother's hand has led me, here her tones fell sadly sweet,
While the storm-birds shoreward surged among the shingle at our feet;
Here she told of manhood's struggles—here she armed me for the strife
I should wage in after years upon the battle-field of Life.
Here she forged the golden chain which links our nature with the skies,
And, from words of Sacred promise, proved the virtuous are the wise.

Ah! my mother! gentler maxims never fell
  from mortal tongue—
Sweeter music never murmured, softer song
  was never sung!
Memories of your kindly face still haunt me
  as in times of yore,
But your foot no more may fall on Illawarra's
  sunny shore.

* * * * * * *

Here among the mountain-mosses, where the
  dazzling days of Youth
Pass'd like splendid phantoms through the
  fairy halls of Love and Truth,
I would rest me while my heart to dreams of
  bygone years returns,
And my burning brow is buried in a leafy lap
  of ferns.

On this lichen'd cedar log, beneath whose
    span the wild creek whirls,
I have sat, and watch'd the landscape, latticed
    by the golden curls
Showering, like mimosa-blooms, in scented
    streams about my breast,
While a trustful cheek turned fondly upward
    from its pillow'd rest.
Watch'd we then the purple vapours climbing
    Kembla's craggy cone—
Like a robe of regal splendor round a rugged
    war-king thrown!
Here we linked the flying hours—heart in
    heart, and hand in hand—
Listening to the far-off music of the meeting
    sea and land—
Listening to the mellow tones that echoed
    from each pleasant word,

Joining with the bell-like chimings of the
 distant dingle-bird.

Ah! I fain would feel that forehead nestling
 on my bosom now!
Ah! I would those curls were rippling like a
 cool wave on my brow!
But the grey-green moss is growing where
 our names once interweaved,
And the myrtle-bark is withered—like the
 face of one deceived!
Lonely! weary! leaden-weighted, let the lag-
 ging hours go by—
O the wealth of Love and beauty lost to
 earth when loved ones die!

* * * * * * *

But though hearts have been divided, and the
  eyes with tears are wet,
Illawarra is unaltered—here the freshness
  lingers yet!
Here the daylight's broken brilliance blazons
  still the broad lagoon;
And the tassell'd maize and forest revel in
  the crimson noon:
Here the grey and grand old mountains rear
  their kingly crowns of gold—
Here the creeks in ancient channels wander
  as in times of old—
Yet, to me, a solemn shadow travels o'er the
  sadden'd plain;
She, who trod the Vale of Darkness, never
  will return again.

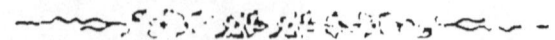

Coming Events.

THE surges were kissing the crags of Kiama,
    The mists of the morning hung heavy and still;
And desolate sea-birds, with sorrowful clamor,
    Wheel'd over the crest of the wind-beaten hill.
Solemnly murmured the voice of the billow
    Down in its darksome and weed-mantled cave,
While a soft, sunny cheek made my bosom its pillow,
    And paled at the weariful wail of the wave!

Sadly the wind sang its deep-sounding chorus,
  Harshly the cavern re-echoed its roar!
And I said, as I thought of the clouds glooming o'er us,
  "Coming events cast their shadows before!"

Up from the depths of the ocean there trembled
  Ruby-like colors that flashed on the foam—
So pure and so bright that their beauty resembled
  The love-smile that welcomes a wanderer home!
The glittering ringlets lay wreathed on my shoulder,
  Like gold-tinted buds of the wild wattle-tree;
And my darling's dear voice, as I turned to behold her.

Chimed softly and sweet with the song of the sea!
"Behold, love!" she whisper'd, "the blushes of morning
Are gilding the heaven that arches us o'er;
We see not the sun, but he heralds his dawning:
'Coming events cast their brightness before!'"

And thus, as we turned from the headland and wandered
Down by the myrtle-trees fringing the beach,
I thought of our sunbeams and shadows, and ponder'd
How wisely the life-cup was mingled to each—

How the storm that we fancy will shatter the flower,
Only tinges its leaves with a livelier glow—
How the rain-cloud that carries the pitiless shower
Also bears in its bosom the beautiful bow!
And so, if we search for life's blessings, we'll find them,
No matter how clouds of Adversity lour—
The sunshine must surely be lurking behind them,
If "coming events cast their shadows before!"

Jamberoo.

Underneath the waving forests, underneath
　the woodland shade,
Watching where the wayward sunbeams thro'
　the wildwoods flash and fade;
I am sitting, lonely-hearted, where the ruddy
　noon-day burns,
Where the wild and weird-like shadows wander
　o'er the wither'd ferns!
Stern and rugged rise the ridges, where the
　scanty grasses creep,
And the rude and rifted ranges guard the
　valley in its sleep!

Where the clouds hang o'er the tree-tops, clinging round the mountain caves,
Like the whiten'd foam of ocean resting on the shuddering waves.
O the starry mosses cluster on the log where oft we sat
Listening to the Minna Murra murm'ring down the marshy flat!

Silence sleepeth in the valley, and the daylight's golden stain
Glimmers on the rude-built cottage, shimmers on the window pane;
And the vagrant winds steal softly thro' the peach-tree by the door,
Rustling like some far-off music rippling on a sandy shore.

And they tell of pleasant faces, loving faces that we knew,
When, in days gone by, we rambled on the hills of Jamberoo!
And I see the misty Past, tho' darkened by a shrouding hand,
As a wave-tossed vessel catches glimpses of the distant land!

Do you still remember when we sat beneath the myrtle tree,
And the future looked as glowing as a sun-illumined sea?
When we sat upon this gnarly log, as I am sitting now,
And the quiet stars peep'd down and quiver'd fondly on your brow?

Ah! methinks I still can faintly hear the song
 you used to sing,
And my heart is yearning homewards, like a
 bird with wearied wing!
True, the wild-bird chaunts as sweetly, and
 the dews as gently fall,
True, the rosebush bends with blossoms trail-
 ing o'er the broken wall;
And the bush-flowers fringe the margin of the
 reedy forest creek,
As when last you stood beside them, with the
 health-glow on your cheek!
But, tho' trees are bending over, and the
 moss clings to the stone,
Tho' the landscape smiles in beauty—now I
 feel I am alone!
Lonely—lonely—weary hearted! sitting, as in
 years before,

List'ning to the Minna Murra moaning past the cottage door,
List'ning to the muffled murmurs of the mountain music, strange,
Sobbing like a frighten'd echo flying down the dusky range!
O, the spring-time gone for ever! O, the days too bright to last!
O, the bitter, bitter Present! O, the happy, happy Past!

The Beach of Wollongong.

"Come! let me take your honest hand!—I
 love its sturdy grasp,
For many a year hath not unnerved or chilled
 its friendly clasp !
Its hearty pressure cheers my soul, and brings
 me, one by one,
A host of bygone dreams, which flash like
 ripples in the sun.
      I see the good old happy time—
        I hear the dear old song
      That chimed in pleasant measure
        On the beach of Wollongong."

"Ah! brother, since I grasped your hand my
 life has been of change;—
Now bright, now black with shadowing clouds,
 like yonder mountain range;
And darker than the heavy wave that rolls
 along the shore
Is still the bitter gloom that hangs my cheerless future o'er:
    For Love has proved a shallow name,
    Disguising foullest wrong,
    Since last we wandered side by side
    The beach of Wollongong.

The sea-sand, drifting far and wide, has o'er
 the graveyard spread,*

---

* Allusion is here made to the burial-ground, situated imme-
diately behind Wollongong Beach, now almost hidden from ob-
servation by drifting sands.

And buries in its snowy folds the long-deserted
dead;
The salt spray flies in foaming wreaths that
on the mounds are thrown,
Where lie the loved of former years, forgotten
and alone:
> But I, upon whose ruddy cheek
> The healthful colors throng—
> Why do I pace, as one forgot,
> The beach of Wollongong?"

"O banish these regrets, and let your thoughts
be forward cast;
Believe—the Future holds a balm for all the
stormy Past:
The sun just bursting from a cloud outspreads
a lovelier sheen,

And never a rainbow shone on earth but rain-
drops fell between!
 The tones of love will sound again,
  And gently float along
 As when in bygone days we roamed
 The beach of Wollongong."

"Ah! I have felt the heavy wheels of Fate above me roll,—

The shaft of envy in my heart—its iron in my soul;—

Have learned how false the smile, the lips, the hearts of seeming friends—

How little worth the glittering dream where hope and fancy blends:

 "Twill form and flash in changeful shapes
  Not born to linger long;

> Then fade, as yon black cloud that fronts
> The beach of Wollongong."

"As yon black cloud?—then turn your gaze across the ocean—look!
The sun is lighting all the page of Nature's glorious book!
Thus years will prove how deathless love when heart to heart is joined,
And Time will try the blackest lie that ever Slander coined:
> The face will wear its olden charm—
> The heart will breathe the song
> It sang in happier days, upon
> The beach of Wollongong.

The brows which frowned will smile again to know your honest worth,

And lips that curled may be the first to tell
    your praise to earth :
For, like yon clouds, our darkest hour with
    ruddiest gold is lined,
And time will bring the metal forth, and leave
    the dross behind.
        Then pierce with Faith's undoubting
            eye
        The veil where shadows throng;
        And life will beam like sunshine
            On the beach of Wollongong."

Terrara.

A MOONLIGHT REVERIE.

Like fluttering birds from their leaf-hidden
    nests,
The pale stars beginneth to scatter;
Shedding silvery charms on the shadowy mists
    That float around dark Coolangatta.*
The river flows bright from its cliff-guarded
    source,
Like Mercy illuming the brow of Remorse!—
And ever it sings, as it speeds on its course,
    A love-song to sleeping Terrara!

---

    * Coolangatta is the native name of a lofty conical hill near the banks of the Shoalhaven.

And O! with what guilty, yet rapturous bliss,
    It hurries away with its booty!
Betraying the flowers with a Judas-like kiss
    Whilst admiring their magical beauty!
The breath of the night-wind hath lingered
    and died
Among the tall reeds by the dark water-side,
But merrily onward the river doth glide
    Where mountains look down on Terrara!

The light of the cottage fires rises and sinks
    With a ruddy, yet glimmering quiver,
On wattles that cling to the tide-fretted brink
    Bowing their heads to the river!
The landscape sleeps on in a beautiful guise,
Like a maiden who dreaming of Paradise lies!
And Love is down-glancing, with joy-beaming
    eyes,
    From his star-jewell'd halls, to Terrara!

O that Life's waters were always as calm
 As the moonbeam that plays on the river!
O that Affection's encircling arms
 Were press'd to our bosoms for ever!
O that its soul-thrilling, silvery touch
Could imprint on each feature a joy-kindled flush,
Bright as the rose-streaks that heavenward rush
 When morning approaches Terrara!

Gerringong.

"Lo! the daylight's glowing splendor branches o'er the reddening skies—
Like the first fond dream of love awakening in a dear one's eyes!
And the morning winds are lowly singing in their lonely caves,
Where the welcome light is weaving rare embroidery on the waves,—
Lighting up the pointed crag-tops—twinkling on the starry spray—
Resting on the tinted ripples creeping up the quiet bay.

Let us walk the beach together—let me clasp
  this gentle hand
While we watch the whisp'ring wavelets surging up the golden sand,—
While we listen to the breezes wandering o'er
  the laughing sea,
Telling to the waves their love-tales—such a
  tale I'd tell to thee!

"Look upon the scene around us—hear the
  water's pleasant chime,
And from emblems let us gather something
  of the future time—
Something which, when cold and chilling
  snows of Age are round us cast,
Will waken into glad remembrance sunny
  moments of the past!

Men have met with disappointments, and have watch'd their hopes depart,
Till the blighted tendrils only clung around the ruin'd heart;
And when thus they look on Nature with mistrustful, doubting eyes,
They can find the rose's thorns, but know not where the fragrance lies.
They may gather sordid treasures, but the precious, priceless gem
Beauty sets on Nature's forehead, shines, but shines in vain for them!
But while life is bright before us shall we idly sit and mourn?
Shall we spurn the flower because its charms are guarded by a thorn?
No! there's beauty—passing beauty—everywhere on earth and sea,

While that bosom beats so fondly—while
those eyes but smile on me.

"True, the flashing waves are brightest where
the shallows lurk beneath—
True, the hidden reef is ever crownēd with a
beauteous wreath;—
But tho' Ocean's smiles are fairest when they
hide the treacherous sand,
Surely I can never doubt the loving pressure
of this hand?
See yon wooded cliff where branches in a wild
embrace enlock—
Where the sunshine's gold and crimson mingle
strangely on the rock,
Till its presence seems to shed a blessing on
the straggling moss :—

Surely tints like these can never hide beneath
them worthless dross!

"I have walked in barren places, toiling on
Life's thorny path—
I have battled with the tempest in its wildest
maddest wrath!
When the night bent o'er the sea and hush'd
the sobbing waves to sleep,
And from out the vessel's wake the pale light
darted on the deep;
When the moonlight glitter'd faintly, I have
stood upon the deck
Building hopes that time engulph'd, as billows
hide a sunken wreck!
Weaving in the loom of Fancy, pictures—
changeful as the clouds—

Soft and dream-like, as the moonshine flickering on the trembling shrouds:
Till a dull, delicious slumber hover'd o'er the wearied brain,
And, thro' tears, glad visions sparkled—like stray sunbeams thro' the rain!

"See! beneath us lies the hollow where the glassy waters sleep—
Where the silver-tinted shell-fish thro' the purple sea-weeds creep;
Sea-flowers spread their pearly petals, waving in the lucent tide,
And the crimson coral branches cling around the rocky side,
Where the spray drops slow and sadly from the cliffs so stern and wild

Gently as a mother's tears that fall upon a
 dying child !
O how sweetly peaceful seems the bosom of
 that mimic sea !
And as pure—believe me, dear one—is the
 love I bear for thee !"

Thus I spake as on we wander'd, and the
 ripples kissed the strand,
Where a flood of golden sunshine shimmer'd
 on the yellow sand ;
Till I deem'd the sounding waters never sang
 so sweet a song
Since the morn when first they trembled
 'neath the cliffs of Gerringong !

Years have pass'd, and Time hath planted deeper furrows on my brow—

O the weary day! how tardy creep the sluggish moments now!—

Lo! a dusky vapour travels from the mountain's darken'd caves,

And the frenzied foam-spots spatter thickly on the surging waves;

For the timid light is lurking, lingering, in the lurid west,

And the storm is wildly trampling on the ocean's tortured breast,

Where the shrieking sea-birds to their cavern'd nests in terror flee

And the ghastly cliffs are glaring fiercely out upon the sea!

O the weary waves so wildly wailing with their weird-like tones!
As their fretful tears are thrown, like scatter'd pearls upon the stones.
O the purple billows bursting on the black and broken reef!
O the dreams as rudely shatter'd! O the dreams as bright—as brief!

Hark! the coming thunder mutters with a strangely boding sound,
Echoing down the distant gully, like the baying of a hound;
And the misty clouds are drifting, where the glimmering lightnings shine—
Ghastly shadows, wildly mingled—even such a life is mine!

Would the tempest's hissing breath could
 dull the wounded spirit's smart !—
Would the rain's remorseful tears could wash
 remembrance from the heart !

Tell me not of warning voices whisp'ring of
 the coming storm—
Sorrow—snake-like—loves to linger where
 the sunshine's wild and warm !
When I rear'd my cloud-wrought castles out
 on Fancy's flowery plain,
Dreamt I of the shatter'd, crumbled, ruin'd
 hopes which now remain ?
Dreamt I, when I sat with her, and marked
 the love-light on her cheek—
That the bliss was but as transient as the sea-
 wave's foamy streak ?

Fool—ay, worse than fool to trust her! how
   I yielded 'neath her wiles—
How I hugged my captive chains because
   they glitter'd in her smiles!
She!—yet, no—I cannot blame her;—when
   the bitter memories press—
When my spirit fain would curse her, then
   my tongue but moves to bless!
And methinks one gentle accent, one forgiv-
   ing word of old,
Could re-waken ancient feelings — feelings
   now so dull and cold!
Could rekindle vanish'd joys, which now the
   changeless Past enlocks—
Joys that flash'd with fire as fickle as the foam
   on yonder rocks!
But she will not turn to bless me; for the low
   sweet dream is o'er,

And the fancy-fashioned fabric fallen—ah!—
    for evermore:
Never—never—never! may we sing again
    love's pleasant song—
"Never!"—hark! the cold waves chiming
    'neath the cliffs of Gerringong!

Poems

OF THE

Australian Bush.

Lost in the Bush.

It lay upon the sand—a shrivelled thing,
    On which the sun in freakish humor slanted;
A lonesome crow above it flapped its wing,
    And o'er the dreary dead a requiem chanted.

All in the rosy rain of summer beams,
    That fell in splendid showers, and changed and shifted,
As (like bright vessels seen in fancy's dreams)
    Across the sea of sky white cloudlets drifted.

Some shreds of rag about the ruin hung,
    To show the ghastly thing had once been human;
And where the skin together scarcely clung
    The bright skull gleamed—the brow once kissed of woman!

A pair of stockman's boots, half filled with sand,
    A saddle, soiled of time and changeful weather,
A blanket hid with fern, a glistening hand
    That held in death the rotten garb together.

The other clutched a faded portrait-case—
    (Some girlish face by memory fondly cherished).
No token of his name or boyhood's place—
    No scrap to tell us when or how he perish'd.

*   *   *   *   *   *

What time the sun its mocking radiance shed,
  Perhaps he died, those stony ridges climbing.
Now a bright creek is tumbling o'er its bed,
  In heedless ears its music idly chiming!

Too late it came—as sweet things often come!—
  As tears that on dead faces fall and glisten—
As when long-lagging tones of kindness hum
  Their words to those who never more may listen.

How many, who have loved and looked in vain

O'er wint'ry fields, and when the bees were
    humming,
Will watch and wait, and look and long again
    To hear the old familiar footsteps coming.

How many ghost-like omens, one by one,
    Will toll their death-knells for the absent
    brother?
And tears for this—perhaps her only son,
    Will wet the lashes of his widowed mother.

Her faith can never fade—*her* hope decay:
    Despair *may* dull the edge of Friendship's
    sorrow;
But she (as wreck'd men watch for break of
    day)
    Awaits his coming with the coming morrow.

The Mountain Moss Spring.

A blacken'd block of crumbling crag where grey-green lichens spread,
Where the wild creek flows in a dream beneath, and mists curl overhead;
And boulders lie at the broken base where a scatter'd brilliance burns,
    And the log—from whence the dingo peeps
    And the timid iguana creeps—
        Is hid in a flush of ferns.

One end hid in their feathery fronds, falling
  with age apart—
The other laid on a bubbling spring, like a
  hand on a beating heart;
Bridging the water's quiet sleep, and glass'd
  in its gleaming face,
    The old log spans the mossy pool,
    While its semblance rests where sha-
  dows cool
        With the sun-flakes interlace.

I sit in a nook of the wild-wood bridge, and
  ponder the golden noon
That flashes and flits in a splendid maze on
  the moss-lined lone lagoon,
Where the wattle whirls its glorious curls from
  out of its tangled wreath,

And the yellow buds of its fragrant flowers
Are floating to fall in drifting showers,
    Like tears, on the pool beneath.

O wondrous peace! that lurks at rest in the mountain's mossy cup,
Where the wet fern droops to meet the kiss of the bubbles sparkling up;
Where sun-tints, caught in a crimson net, on the glistening pebbles glow,
    And purple plumes, to the rocks that cling,
    Are nodding their heads, and seem to sing
        With the waters, sweet and low!

O gentle peace!—O wondrous calm!—would
  I might own your sway,
And the depths of my feverish heart be still,
  as the pool in its rocks of grey!
For the wattle-blooms will come once more
  to mix with the summer fern—
    But the love that falls, like a golden
      bud,
    To wander at will on a wayward
      flood,
        Will never again return!

Waiting for the Mail.

Breaks a sun-streak through the casement—
streams its glory on the floor,
And the crisp and matted leafage rustles
round the cottage door;
Where the truant buds are climbing,
Tapping on the glass, and chiming
With the sounding burst of billows breaking
on the shingly shore!

Watching by the open window where the
starry blossoms cling—
Listening to the weary song the weeping
waters ever sing—

Sad and thoughtful, sits a maiden,
For her peaceless breast is laden
With the wish for news of one whose memory
makes the tear-drop spring.
So she watches where the sun is fading on a
distant sail—
Where the scattered sea-spray drifts and tosses
in the summer gale,
And her girlish heart is throbbing
Like the cold wave's ceaseless sobbing:
O! for weary Youth and Beauty—waiting,
waiting for the Mail.

Let us track the steps so long'd-for, o'er the
parched Australian plain—
Mark the spot that heard the raving death-
calls of his thirsty pain!

See the ironbark, unalter'd
Sheds its leaves where footsteps fal-
ter'd—
Footfalls that shall never greet the watchful
glance of Love again!

When wild dreams of brattling creeks thrust
in his ears their phantom tones,
Here he fell, and clutched for water at the
burning sand and stones,
Till the tortured spirit wrestled
Forth its flight—then 'possums nestled
In the branches, shyly wondering at the heap
of brightening bones!

There he sleeps—and mouldering rags are
wasting in the heated gale—

Peering from the drifting sand, they flutter forth a fearful tale.
> Love may watch and wait for ever,
> But the wish'd-for voice will never

Tremble in the ear of her who watches— waiting for the Mail!

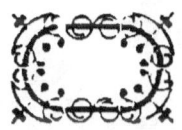

Arakoon.*

BRUSH SCENERY ON THE MACLEAY.

Frighted night hath left her jewels clinging
    to each shivering bough,
And the ruddy morn's reflection gildeth Ara-
    koon's dark brow—
Skimmering over matted ferns, and streaming
    with its restless fires,
On the glist'ning granite ranges—flickering
    on their rocky spires—
Peering down some dark-faced crevice, where
    the sluggish waters glide,

---

    * Arakoon is the aboriginal name of a lofty hill at the mouth of the Macleay River.

And the purple vapours hover round the cavern's dripping side;
Where the timorous grass-tree, trembling, hangs above the fretted steep,
Shudd'ring as it hears below it waters moaning in their sleep.

Here the moistful mosses cluster on a fallen forest trunk,
Where the sunshine, thro' the branches, to the dreamy earth has sunk:
And the starry-blossomed creeper—feeding on the trunk's decay,
Waves aloft its flowery crest, and triumphs in the light of day.
See! the quivering gold is dancing on the solemn dark-leaved pines,

And the interwoven wood-buds glitter in their
 chain of vines.
Arakoon! the tree ferns revel in the clefts
 that gash thy sides,
Creeping upward till the fog-wreath all their
 wild-wood beauty hides.

But thy peak, with seer-like warning, ever
 points to realms above,
Teaching with a voiceless fervor lessons of
 confiding love :
Sitting in thy mateless sorrow with a tearless
 look of grief,
Thrusting forth thy suppliant arms, and spurn-
 ing all the world beneath.
I have stood where rock-chained waters
 struggled from their prison den,

List'ning to the spirit-voices chanting down the distant glen—
Syren-voices—air-drawn phantoms—trooping from their mountain hall,
Luring on the thoughtless ripples to the foam-enshrouded fall.

O! the tide look'd so enchanting when its waves went singing by;
Blossoms sprang to kiss its bosom—tempted thus to kiss and die:
And the river rushed delighted with the lovely freight it bore—
Murmuring forth a gentle prelude to the torrent's dashing roar.
And again I traced the waters stealing on by ferny banks,

Where the spiry reeds were nodding as the
    wind crept through their ranks;
And the clear translucent pools, unruffled by
    a passing breath,
Slept in rocky hollows, silent as the surfless
    tide of death.

Now I watch the moss-fringed lakelets drink-
    ing in the summer-shine—
O their eyes, so bright and tearful, glancing
    fondly into mine!—
Now I follow, till the waters, blushing in the
    light of Noon,
Steal, with soft and gentle murmurs, past the
    hill of Arakoon—
Where the rank and wayward grasses over
    rugged fissures stray

Till their green and waving blades are silver'd by the salt sea spray.
O the river's gleesome singing when it meets its friend—the sea!
Waken's deep responsive music—bringeth many a joy to me!

One by one the sunny sparkles, bubbling in the cup of Hope,
Flash upon its ruddy surface—like the light on yonder slope!
Darting with a fearless vigor into Life's vast treasure-mine—
Where the dross of vice lies festering—where the gems of beauty shine!
For, since man first drank of sorrow, Pleasure shares the world with pain—

Breezes mingle with the tempest—sunshine follows after rain:
Even tears of weeping darkness form the gems that grace the leaf,
And the very wings of sorrow, flapping, cool the brow of Grief.

Sunset in the Forest.

The swamp-nurtured vapors are heavenward
    creeping,
  Like a treacherous band on the trail of a foe
Where verdureless ranges, their weary watch
    keeping,
  Look jealously down on the gullies below:
The night-owl's sad notes through the forest
    are knelling,
  The curlew sails o'er with a shuddering shriek;
And, borne like a sigh on the night-wind,
    comes swelling

The low, smothered sob of the rain-swollen creek!
    On the night-wind comes swelling
    The low smothered sob of the rain-swollen creek!

Darkly and drearily—dusk-shadows, flying,
  Clamber the ridges where fog-wreaths are curled—
Dusky and dreamy—the daylight is dying—
Wasting away from the desolate world!
The yellow light shimmers on rude mountain ledges—
  O! that a love-glance so tender and bright
Should smile on the clouds and illumine their edges,
  Then leave them enclasped in the dark arms of Night!

Illumine their edges,
Then leave them enclasped in the dark arms of Night!

Rifted and shattered, the rugged clouds scatter—
Paler the flush on the western sky burns;
Slowly and sadly the heavy drops patter,
Falling like tears on the feathery ferns.
But far in the east, over storm-splintered ridges,
All heart-full of love comes the beautiful moon,
To silver the sedge—where the fallen log bridges
The deep solemn sleep of the quiet lagoon!
The fallen log bridges
The deep solemn sleep of the quiet lagoon.

And thus—in the wearisome path of existence,
  When friends, one by one, fall away from the gaze—
As vessels grow dreamy and dim in the distance
  Till their masts seem to mingle and melt in the haze!
O! then thy dear voice, like the song of a fairy,
  Seems filling the world with sweet music for me!—
One pale little flower can enliven the prairie—
  My life is enlivened by smiles, love, from thee!
    O for the happiness!—
    O for the happiness centred in thee!

Such is the Way of the World.

I LAY where the forest was flinging
    Its frowns on the summer-dyed earth,
And the mountain creek gaily was singing
    A song to the scene of its birth;—
Where it paced among pinnacles hoary,
    With a soft and melodious tread—
Then flash'd in its sun-dazzled glory—
    A tangled but silvery thread.

And yet its pure waters seemed lonely,
    Attracting no worshipping throng;
For the love-tale which greeted it only
    Was the dingle-bird's eloquent song.

Each reed that waved restlessly over,
    And bent o'er the verge of the creek,
Turned away like a renegade lover,
    To press its slim leaves to my cheek.

The dark *casurinas** o'er-arching,
    Look'd scornfully silent and still:
But onward the river kept marching
    From its home to the forest-clad hill.
Unheeding the scowl of the wildwood—
    For virtue is proof against fears—
It sped like a vision of childhood,
    Enshrouded in sunshine and tears.

And thus—like that chaste mountain torrent,
    So rich, yet so seemingly poor—

---

* The Swamp Oak *Casurina Palludosa.*

Humble worth seemeth ever abhorrent,
    No matter how virtuously pure.
It may lovingly sue for affection,
    But backward it ever is hurl'd,
Beneath the harsh scowl of rejection—
    For such is the way of the world.

A storm-splintered trunk was upflinging
    Its form in the summer-flushed air;
And dark vines around it were clinging
    Like the tear-nourished weeds of despair.
Its limbs bore no vocalists merry,
    But painfully downwards did turn,
As tho' they were yearning to bury
    Their shame in the shadowy fern.

The leaf-thwarted sunbeams were streaming
    Thro' the foliage grappling above;

And on the pale bush blossoms gleaming
    Seem'd pressing a fond kiss of love.
And then they resplendently floated
    Where a sluggish pool weed-mantled lay,
And turn'd up its features—slime-bloated,
    To the gaze of the glorious day.

Its surface was lit with a lustre
    That seem'd in its transient pride,
To spurn the rich golden-plum'd cluster
    The wattles had shower'd at its side.
But it courted the insects which hover'd
    And flashed in its radiant glow,
And worshipp'd the beauty that cover'd
    The worthlessness hidden below.

Like that stagnant pool, brightly reclining,
    And the frail borrow'd brilliance it bore—

Wherever wealth's candle is shining,
　　There are myriad moths who adore!
On folly's void meaningless features
　　Let the impress of wealth be impearl'd—
There are plenty will worship the creature—
　　For such is the way of the world.

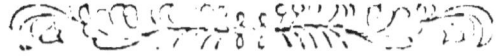

Sea-side Lyrics.

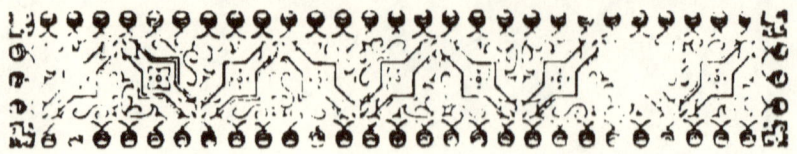

Floating Away.

Where the tremulous wave is upheaving
   To catch the last glance of the west,
The summer-shine softly is weaving
   A robe for its beautiful breast.
The shivering brilliance is lying
   On the sails of the ships in the bay;
But, like smiles from the lips of the dying,
   Its glory is wasting away!
      Stealing a kiss from the fisherman's skiff
      As it darts from the arms of the sheltering cliff,

Where the rock-shattered billows are
 moaning, as if
For the foam-bubbles floating away!

O! the heart-pulses quicken their throbbing,
 At thoughts of the voices of yore;
Recalled by the sorrowful sobbing
 Of the sea, as it beats on the shore.
O! it bears, in the song it is singing,
 A dream of that beautiful day
When the heart, to the fond Present clinging,
 Never dreamt of the Future's decay!
  When the days that we knew were all
   dazzle and gleam,
  Like the sunshine and shade of some
   fanciful dream,
  Till, like withered leaves dropt in a
   fast-flowing stream,
  Our life-blossoms floated away :

Since we sat 'neath yon headland together,
    And heard the sea's musical song;
Thro' Life's ever-varying weather
    We have drifted, and drifted along.
When we watch'd till the moonlight was sleeping
    In the arms of the rock-girdled bay,
And reck'd not of night-shadows creeping
    To darken the light of our day.
        O! it may be a folly, but never a crime,
        To think with regret of that happiest time
        When the heart and its yearnings were both in their prime,
        Ere our boyhood's dreams floated away!

St. Valentine's Eve.

St. Valentine's Eve! how my heart-pulses quiver
  For happy days gone, like a wave from the beach,
When the whisper of winds, and the rush of the river,
  Awaken sweet memory's dreams into speech!
They bring back a tale of affection requited,
  They linger, like sun-streaks, reluctant to leave,
And tell of the time when with feelings united
  We rambled the shore on St. Valentine's Eve!

Honey-birds loiter'd to suck at the wattle,
   And parrots flashed forth with their feathers of fire!
Where the leaf-broken light was beginning to mottle
   A magical net-work on brushwood and briar.
Down in the cedar-glen creepers were clinging,
   Tossing their shining bells, tender and sweet;
While the rustle of reeds, and the hidden creek's singing,
   Mingled their sounds with the fall of our feet!
And I thought that the star-blossoms shaking above me

With crimson and green might a garland
    enweave;
But, with light on my path, and a loved one
    to love me,
A brighter I wove on St. Valentine's Eve!

We turned from the bush-track that ran with
    the river,
And led thro' the tea-tree scrub belting the
    strand;
Where footsteps made music that chimed
    with the shiver
Of white-curling billows that surged o'er
    the sand.
Softly the swamp-oak, in wild whispers wail-
    ing,
Mutter'd its sorrows to her and to me;

While the ruddier glare of the daylight was
paling,
And a shadow crawled forth, like a frown
on the sea !
But the darkest of clouds could not sorrow
or sadden
The light of my soul, for I said, " Shall I
grieve,
When love-glancing eyes turn to solace and
gladden,
And heart beats to heart on St. Valentine's
Eve ?"

Ah ! many a season has come and evanished
Since rock-pool and cavern awoke with our
tread !
The laughter that cheer'd them for ever is
banished,

The eyes that look'd on them are faded
and dead.
The clustering vine may entangle its branches,
And scatter its beautiful buds as before;
And the gurgle and gush, where the shallow
wave glances,
Fall flute-like and faint on the ripple-worn
shore.
But I turn with a sigh of regret from the Pre-
sent,
And still to the sweet-bitter Past I would
cleave;
For Memory's rainbow gleams softly and
pleasant
Thro' the sunshine and shade of St. Valen-
tine's Eve!

Under the Cliffs.

Let us wander near the headland where the sluggish surges crawl,
And the wayward waves are wildly clutching at the cavern'd wall;
Let us, hand in hand with Memory, watch the fisher's flashing skiff,
Where the white sails spot the purple waters wailing 'neath the cliff—
Sobbing o'er the shining shingle, where the scanty grasses grow,
And our names were rudely carved—ay! more than twenty years ago.

Warring winds and restless rainings stole like
    shadows up the strand,
And the heaps of batter'd sea-wrack grovelled
    in the drifting sand;
So we found that storms had stained the
    stone where once we loved to trace
Each well-known name, till grain by grain
    they faded from its faithless face!

Sit beside me, gentle sister—(more you never
    were to me)—
Sit beside me now, and listen to the sadness
    of the sea;
While the waves are surging landward, and
    the beach is fringed with foam,
Let the tides of fond affection flood and flow
    from heart to home.

While the vines are swinging o'er us, and the
    soft winds flush your cheek,
Let us revel in the future, and of days evan-
    ished speak.

Do you still remember when we strolled
    adown the leafy lane,
When the broken brilliance flitted through
    the branches bowed with rain,
When your eyes were bright with passion,
    when your lips with love were warm,
And your face was like the weather, half of
    sunshine, half of storm?
Ah! I mind me how I pleaded that our lives
    might interweave,
Like the twining buds above us on that
    changeful summer's eve;

But with girlish pride you pouted, fearing to
   be quickly won ;
And my hopes were dulled and dead in concert with the sinking sun.
How you hinted of *another*, spoke with tears
   of " parting vows,"
Till my lids with anguish trembled, like the
   rain-drops on the boughs.
So we parted. You, to grace the fireside of
   a favored swain—
I, to fight alone and friendless, on the world's
   great battle-plain.

※   ※   ※   ※

Time, that stern, yet kind magician, waved
   ⁂ ⁂ ⁂ ⁂ ⁂ ⁂ ⁂ ⁂ ⁂ ⁂
Rolling out their silver linklets—yours of love,
   and mine of tears !

Summer eves before me flit in all the gladsome garb of yore,
Like the welcome wash of waters on an old familiar shore :
Thought flies back to thought, as vessels on the ocean-highways meet ;
Memories greet, like well-known faces flashing through a crowded street.

Many days since then have told their numbers forth with passing breath,
Many nights have laid them down and slept the wakeless sleep of death ;
And the loved and trusted with the happy days of Spring have flown,
Leaving us, like mountain-summits in the weary night. alone !

I have panted for a touch no stranger's fingers
    could possess,
I have fought in dreams to clutch the hand I
    now so fondly press;
I have felt, in strange wild visions, arms of
    old around me cast,
O the light that breaks upon me! Truth
    and Love unite at last!

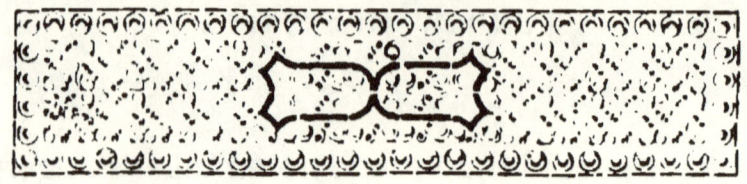

Voices from the Sea.

See! the bashful shades are hiding,
And the morning mist dividing,
Shows the 'frighted stream that tumbles
   Down the rocks that gird the bay;
Where the waves are wild and foamy—
And the headland, moist and loamy,
Like an ancient ruin—crumbles,
   Lone and dreary, to decay!

O, the sea-bells, faintly chiming!
O, the truant blushes climbing,
Where the stars look pale and weary,
   As they close their dreamy eyes!

And the golden rays are creeping
Where the sun, in splendour sweeping,
Like an eagle from his eyrie,
   Soareth to the ruddy skies.

O, I love the changeful ocean!
And a kindred, strange emotion
Cometh, as I gaze to seaward,
   Like a song of life to me!
Like a blind girl's fingers straying
Over harp-strings, softly playing
Fitful music, wild and wayward—
   Cometh voices from the sea!

Let us sit where mournful mosses
Cluster on the rock that crosses
O'er the valley, green and grassy,
   Stretching down to meet the waves;

Where they quiver, flush'd and gleamy,
And a murmur soft and dreamy,
Underneath the surface glassy,
   Gurgles in the slimy caves!

O ye mourner, weary-hearted!
Sighing for the long-departed;
Voices from the sea-waves whisper
   Songs of bygone years to thee!
How on sunny shores ye rambled,
Where the laughing wavelets gamboll'd,
And ye heard the loved one lisp her
   Tales of gladness by the sea!

Where are all the vows we utter'd,
As the restless sea-birds flutter'd,
And the idle winds were rushing
   Past the ragged cliffs above!

Where are now the curls that shiver'd
In the breeze—the lips that quiver'd,
And the cheek with transport blushing,
   As we told our boyhood's love?

O 'tis sweet, 'tis sweet to nourish
Flowers of Love! and as they flourish,
Twine the blooming buds together—
   Leaf and tendril—round the heart!
But 'tis sad to see them perish,
Watch the hopes we fain would cherish,
In their beauty pine and wither,
   Feel them one by one depart!

Earthly bliss is transient only—
O the bitter world, and lonely!
We have quaffed the draught of gladness
   We may never taste again!

For the rosy drops are scatter'd,
For the very cup is shatter'd,
And the dreary shade of sadness
Cometh ever in our train!

Footprints in the Sand.

The headlands force their rifted peaks
  Through scanty garbs of green,
Where muttering waves are spread before,
  And the white beach lies between :
The billows trail their surfy fringe
  Over the shining strand—
Ever crooning a sweet refrain,
They drift from shore and return again,
Washing away with their sparkling rain
  Our footprints from the sand !

The fig-tree casts a pleasant shade
  On the straggling ferns below,
And the tea-scrub lines the shadowy creek
  Where the sea-waves ebb and flow :
The shells are crushed by a tiny foot,
  And I clasp a trustful hand ;
While forward the flashing foam-streaks leap,
Or slyly over the sand-bar creep,
And, as we wander, the waters sweep
  Our footprints from the sand.

O never a footstep trod the sand
  That beaches Life's sea-shore,
But the waves of Death have hid the strand,
  And the much-loved marks it bore :
The trace of the child who fled from the sea
  That wasted the crumbling land ;

The steps of lovers skirting the bay,
The feeble marks of the old and grey,
The waters of Time have washed away
    Their footprints from the sand !

The shore we tread is a changeful one,
    And, heedless of prayer or vow,
The tide of years will efface the marks
    We treasure with fondness now ;
But ever we'll travel Life's ocean-side
    Lovingly hand in hand ;
Then whether the ripple shall gently glide,
Or the billow dash in its angry pride,
O may they at once and together hide
    Our footprints in the sand !

Bondi.

Softly moaneth Bondi's waters in their
    jagged storm-wrought caves,
Cowering from the ardent sunbeams blazon'd
    on the tinctured waves;
Far below the toppling cliffs, around their
    foam-clad feet they creep,
Whisp'ring to their giant hearers records of
    the writhing deep.
    Then from out the dull recesses
        Rush they, as with fear oppress'd;
    Fleeing from the coast's caresses,
        Back to Ocean's throbbing breast!

Mutter'd sounds of wrath come trembling
from the sea-wave's curling lips,
As they snatch the pensile spray that from
the darkling cavern drips ;
Then again from shore retreating with a wild
and timorous look,
Till the deep lies half-unravell'd—Nature's
undecipher'd book !
    And the sea's dark floor, weed garnish'd,
      Glittering in the sunlight lies
    Like a palace pavement—burnished
      With the smile of tropic skies !

I have stood where lucid rock-pools glim-
mer'd under Bondi's crags,
Slumbering, like to sleeping infants, guarded
by witch-featured hags !
Where the crimson tinctured sea flowers, twining in a graceful wreath,

Quiver'd o'er the gilded fretwork mirror'd on
the rock beneath.
 O! so peacefully they slumber'd,
  Pure as angel smiles of love—
 Guiding one, whose hours are number'd,
  To the mystic world above!

Thoughts come crowding as I linger gazing
on the blue-robed main,
Like the vaguely-imaged phantoms trooping
thro' a madman's brain;
But the breath of recollection fast dissolves
the shrouding screen;
And the lustrous lamp of memory gleameth
o'er life's fitful scene.
 Like yon wand'ring bird emerging
  From the ocean depths obscure—
 So across my mind come surging
  Visions beautiful and pure.

And I see again before me one who shared
    each smile and tear,
And methinks the silvery cadence of her gen-
    tle voice I hear,
Feel her clinging on my bosom, and her
    warm breath fan my cheeks
Soft as summer winds that rustle down mi-
    mosa-shadow'd creeks.
    She has gone—but memory ever
        Bids the lovely phantom rise:
    Death's cold shaft each heart may sever,
        But remembrance never dies!

Still I view the scene, and yet her fairy form
    before me flits—
Oh, how strong the links of love that round
    our hearts affection knits!

Never may each bright illusion be effaced
    from memory's page,
Tho' the body lose its vigor, and the eye be
    dimm'd with age!
    Still the scenes with love invested
        Come in garbs they ever wore—
    Restless as the billows crested,
        Thrown on Bondi's rugged shore!

Miscellaneous Poems.

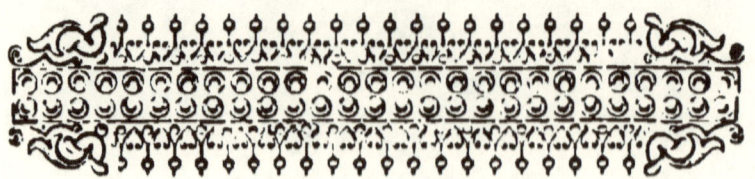

Old Memories.

As one who treads some towering mountain-ridge,
    Watches the wild creek winding thro' the stubble,
As he who, halting on a river bridge,
    Scans with an idle look each eddying bubble—

So stand I, watching, as before my gaze
    Float forms and faces linked with days of childhood;

Breaking like sunshine through the shifting
    haze
That sadly drapes the beauty of the wild-
    wood.

It needs no wizard's skill, no sorcerer's spell,
    To brighten tints by time and distance
    faded ;
They rest in some neglected drawer, and
    dwell
    In withered flowers—in curls with ribbons
    braided :

They peep and peer from unexpected nooks,
    Between the dusk and when the lamps are
    lighted ;
They lurk in memories of words and looks,
    And often come, tho' welcome, uninvited.

They build like birds beneath our household
    eaves,
    Braving the wintry winds that rave and
        wrestle;
And one sweet song, where love with love
    enweaves,
    Will start them forth from corners where
        they nestle!

As I stand here the shadows gather round,
    The sun's bright rim dips in a sea of glory
The sea-winds croon, and mingled with their
    sound
    I hear the music of an old, old story.

The pages of the volume that I bear,
    Link'd with a name whose echo fondly
        lingers,

Flutter and ripple, and a wisp of hair
   Twines like a golden serpent round my fingers.

The yellow threads with sudden tears are wet—
   (When I am gone will others thus regret me?)
And, bound with silk, are words of pearl inlet—
   " Never," the simple sentence runs, " forget me!"

Forget you! when each wave that on the shore
   Falls with a murmur as of distant thunder,

Forgets to roll with long-resounding roar
    Through yon wild gap that keeps the cliffs
        asunder.

Yea, tho' my recollection then should fade,
    And time essay the golden chain to sever,
Still, like a sound by far-off waters made,
    A faint refrain will whisper, " Never —
        never!"

Drowned.

A RUSH of the rain-swollen river,
    A twirl of the treacherous tide—
A girl, with a sigh and a shiver,
    Peers over the dark water-side:

She flits from the lamp's crimson glory,
    And shudders and shrinks from its light—
A girl with a sorrowful story
    Is miss'd from the fireside to-night!

She stands in the shadows, so lonely—
    In the tangle of cordage and spar;

She watches the cloud-rifts, where only
    Looks down, on the sinner, a star.

    *   *   *   *

Steal on, past the glare of the city—
    A terrible secret you own,
Oh, river! Gaze, star, in your pity—
    You shine on the ripples alone!

To-morrow, a crowd will assemble
    To wonder, and whisper, and weep:
Their words will fall softly, and tremble,
    As fearful of breaking her sleep!

They'll carefully smooth out the tresses
    Now twined in her delicate hands;

And straighten the arm that impresses
    Its form in the slime and the sands.

That hand with its cold rigid fingers,
    The pressure of Friendship hath felt—
Those limbs (where the lapping tide lingers)
    At the feet of a mother have knelt.

Ah! she had much of the merit
    That mingles, like gold, with our clay;
But the love that she yearned for in spirit
    Ebb'd, like a cold river, away.

A mother will mourn for a daughter,
    A father will rave for his loss—
The treasure has fled, and the water
    Will leave but the beautiful dross.

Rush on, then, oh, river! in sorrow,
Drearily over the drowned—
Some one has gone, and to-morrow,
Somebody here will be found!

The Stranded Boat.

A RIVER-SIDE REVERIE.

I STAND and watch the daylight cast
   Its death-glance o'er the western range ;
The crimson lights are fading fast,
   The yellow splendours swiftly change.

And, as I watch, my heart is filled
   With dreams of days that long have fled ;
With smiles that linger yet, to gild
   The faces of the memoried dead !

I see the dull reflected glare
   That seems to mock the coppery sky ;

Where, glassy as a drowned man's stare,
    The outward tide slides slowly by.

The crimson clutches crag and tree,
    And, crumbling, falls from leaf to leaf,
Or glints upon the mimic sea
    That eddies round the headland reef.

The faithless waves have left the strand
    And rocks where beaded sea-plants cling ;
And sadly o'er the bare brown sand
    Their lines the gaunt grey shadows fling.

I mark them all—the wafted weeds
    Which idly down the river float ;
The shell-grown stake, the briny reeds,
    Where rests the stranded fisher-boat.

THE STRANDED BOAT.

Left of the waves that kissed its prow,
    And press'd with passion'd lips its planks,
It rests alone!—deserted now
    By waters fondling far-off banks.

O saddening eve! O stranded boat!
    Ye limn a lesson all may learn:
Down Life's dusk stream how many float,
    Who never, never shall return!

Like bubbles on a rainy tide,
    In Time's bleak shades they disappear;
While, stranded by the river-side,
    We lie in mateless sorrow here.

O lonely boat! when sunbeams burn
    In broken fires from bough to bough,

The truant waves will then return
    And plead forgiveness round thy prow;

But we!—the storms of life may drift
    Their sandy wrecks to heap us o'er;
But O for one sweet face to lift
    The cloud that glooms for evermore!

For one fond lip to press our own,
    One breath to mingle with our breath—
When in the ear shall sound alone
    The ripples on the beach of Death!

But vain the prayer—we only see
    Some footprints fading from the shore,
To hint the cheerless years to be,
    To mock the days that are no more!

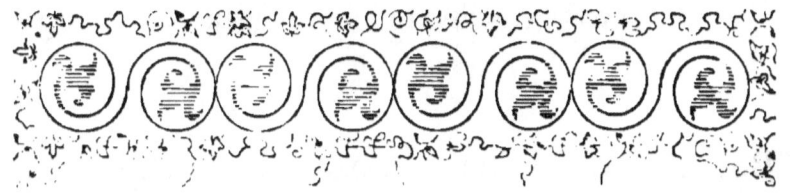

Two Australian Pictures.

(A TRIBUTE TO THE MEMORY OF CAPT. COOK.)

Scene I.—*The Landing of Captain Cook,*
1770.

Fiercely sang the white-lipped surges ; and the echoes of their thunder
  Fled among the ragged caverns glaring on the restless main ;
And the craggy headlands, by the jealous waves, were kept asunder,
  Like the gulf which parts for ever friends who may not meet again.

But the quiet bay, those cliffs defended,
    sparkled in its splendour,
And the surf-drops spread their silvery net-
    work o'er the dazzling sand—
Where, like loving speeches, formed of ac-
    cents O so sweetly tender !
Came the pleasant sound of waters meet-
    ing with the willing land.

Shone the sun in noonday glory, while the
    white clouds hung between it
    And the earth, where light and shade in
    fond embraces seem'd to cling ;
And a pleasing darkness fell athwart the
    scene, as if to screen it
    With a chastened beauty—like the shadow
    of an angel's wing.

From the gunyahs 'neath the headland, curled the smoke, in circles drifting
   Round the branches, where the gum-trees ghastly shadows downward threw
On the water's glassy bosom, where the idle sun-streaks shifting,
   Mirror'd forth the dark-skinned native fishing in his bark canoe.

Scarce a sound disturbed the silence—only when the wild-dog, creeping
   Through the tangled thicket, roused the parrot's harsh discordant scream ;
For the bays and beaches, in each other's arms, were fondly sleeping,
   And the pure Australian sky bent o'er the landscape's lovely dream.

Came a batter'd vessel thro' the harbor-portal, and the rattle
Of her web-like cordage mingled with the murmurs of the breeze;
While her strained and creaking timbers told of many a hard fought battle
With the wild and warring tempests, wandering over weary seas.

And her crew gazed from the bulwarks—but no hand, in love extended,
Sought to give the grasp of friendship to the toiling way-worn band :
No dear voice, in pleasant whispers, spoke of pain and peril ended,
As the rusty cable grated, and the anchor pierced the sand.

No fond mother's grateful blessing hailed this
   " Wanderer of the Ocean"—
No responsive feeling heightened beauty
   on a fair one's cheek ;
And the land contained no manly heart that
   throbbed with wild emotion
At the sight of dear Old England's standard
   floating at her peak.

*But the jealous natives fled, their bosoms
   filled with fear and wonder—
Only two, with patriotic love, remained to
   guard the strand ;

---

* This was the actual reception of the great navigator, who thus describes the circumstance :—" As soon as we approached the rocks, two of the men came down upon them to dispute our landing, and the rest ran away. * * * They brandished their weapons, and seemed resolved to defend their coast to the uttermost, though they were but two, and we were forty. I could not but admire their courage."

And their fierce dissonant yells came wafted
 with the wild wave's thunder,
As the gallant leader placed his foot upon
 the unknown land.

*   *   *   *   *

Scene II.—*Botany Bay*, 1870.

A century has passed—and merry footsteps
 twinkle on the sod ;
But that hardy band of voyagers down a
 stranger path hath trod—
Down a path whose mystic windings cross
 the Future's viewless plain,
On whose waste the foot once planted never
 may return again.

True, the spot is little altered—Nature wears
    the look of yore,
But the savage yell no longer echoes round
    the quiet shore.
Where the wild man loved to urge his bark
    canoe amid the spray,
Now a cloud of white-winged skiffs are dart-
    ing o'er the placid bay—
Now the sound of pleasant voices comes like
    bells upon the ear,
And the eager heart beats swifter as some
    loved one draweth near.
O the tinted wings of Fancy!—how they bear
    us to the skies,
As we read our happy fate in glances shot
    from beaming eyes!
Whilst the youthful laugh re-echoes, as we
    wander hand in hand—

Full of music as the deep-toned fall of waves
upon the sand!
But while Pleasure flies before us, let our
thoughts be backward cast,
Let our grateful memories turn the glorious
pages of the Past;
Where the annals of our country to admiring
eyes unfold
All the simple faith and courage of those gallant men of old!
Shall we rear the marble pile to him, who,
with his Cain-like frown,
Thro' the blood-red field of battle wades to
grasp a victor's crown?
Shall we call him "great" whose fame is built
on wretched captives' fears,
And whose very triumphs float upon some
ruined nation's tears?

While we pass, as if unseen, the leader and his fearless band,
Who brought those smiling angels—Peace and Commerce—to our native land?
We may sound a thousand praises—we may tune a thousand songs—
But to hero-efforts better, deeper praise than this belongs!
E'en while they tremble on our lips, our words but live to pass away,
And the stone which bears a hero's name must crumble to decay.
But, my country, let us prove—while willing Memory backward darts—
That the record of brave actions lives for ever in our hearts!

Shadows on the Wall.

While years press on to their misty bourne,
   my soul to their shadow clings,
As a sea-bird grasps at the passing wave that
   rolls beneath its wings !
For tho' the links of Memory's chain are dim
   with a thousand tears,
My throbbing brain would fain retain a
   glimpse of vanished years !
    The mingled web that the Past enweaves,
      I would remember all ;
    Each sunbeam resting on the leaves,
      Each shadow on the wall !

A garden wall—and twinkling buds in starry
   clusters shake ;
Where shivering shafts of golden light through
   bending branches break ;
And the tinkling gush of laugh and shout
   thro' the merry greenwood darts,
As Pleasure's fingers touch the chords that
   dwell in childish hearts !
   O a vain, vain prayer from my bosom
      slips,
      That ever I might recall
   The clustering curls and meeting lips
      Now shadowed on the wall !

A sea-washed wall that fronts the bay where
   ships their canvas furl,
Where feathery foam-flakes fringe the beach,
   and surfy billows curl ;

There youthful hearts and loving lips renew
their child-love's bond,
And Mercy hides the wreck-strewn shore that
stretches far beyond!
 O, warm the love that fires his breast!
 O, fair her tresses fall!
 And a nestling head to a bosom prest
 Is shadowed on the wall!

A broken wall—the mossy stones with ivy
fetters bound,
Where the ghostly rays of moonlight rest
upon the leafy ground!
Some years have passed, and they who tread
those ferny paths have tried,
And tested fond Affection's links to find them
still abide!

The light that shudders from above
On wrinkling brows may fall;
But, O, a world of deathless love
Is shadowed on the wall!

A cottage wall—where fire-gleams dance, and ruddy glares are thrown,
And yet, a mocking, barren place, where my shadow rests—alone!
O heart! to think of the joy that *was*—of the gloom that still must *be!*
Of the whiten'd wall, and the lonely shade that ever is turned to me!
O summer sun, you may smile as bright,
But never may you recall
The dear dead face your gladsome light
Once shadowed on the wall!

Advance Australia.

Advance, advance Australia! The Peaceful
   and the Free!
The wide world holds no truer hearts than
   ours which beat for thee!
Reared where thy crested ridges lift their bold
   brows to the sky,
Or where the wild creek ploughs thy sod, or
   brattles idly by—
Nurtured beneath the flashing beams that
   gild thy girdling foam,
Our inmost hearts still link with thine the
   magic name of " home!"

Still, still we hold Australia the dearest spot on earth,
And prize above all boasted lands the country of our birth!

Thy infant annals may not blaze with tales of battle deeds,
To bid the cheek of Pity pale, and dim the eye that reads;
No cloud of carnage sheds upon thy fields its crimson rain,
No steel-carved lays of savage strife thy peaceful records stain,
Thy free flag lifts its starry cross, and, scorning class or clan,
It loves to float above the head of every honest man.

Pure as thine own unsullied skies long may it
fondly wave
Its folds around each true-born son, and flout
each traitor-knave!

The rose is twined for the dear Old Land
our fathers call their own,
And flowers for hue and fragrance famed
have emblem'd many a throne;
But thou—our own Australia!— Queen of the
Southern Sea!
What blooms shall bind thy glittering locks?
what shall we wreathe for *thee?*
We'll twine the golden-tassel'd maize, the
myrtle, and the vine,
With treasures of the ripened wheat, and call
the chaplet thine!

With prayers for all thy future good we'll
  place it on thy brow,
And shout " Advance Australia !" and sing
  " God speed her plough !"

Advance, advance Australia ! a meed of nobler praise
Than trumpet-notes of ruthless strife our
  loving lips shall raise.
Born to restore the nations to a brotherhood
  of peace,
To bind the wounds by Faction made—bid
  curse of creeds to cease ;
To cause the failing fires of faith to brightly
  burn again,
And feed the famished tribes of earth with
  thine abundant grain !

Such ever be thy children's aims where'er thy sunbeams fall,
So shall " Advance Australia!" be a watch-word for us all!

God bless our Sailor Prince.

AN AUSTRALIAN TRIBUTE.

March, 1868.

A CLOUD hath come over the light of our land,
A gloom hath o'ershadowed its splendour;
And, like the low wailing of waves on the sand.
 Fall whispered tones—mournful and tender ;
For warm hearts are filled with affectionate fears,
And eyes—bright with hopes of youth's happiest years—

Now bear on their lashes the traces of tears,
    Bespeaking the grief of Australia!

The prayers of the agèd—the shouts of the young—
    Intermingled with loving devotion;
And our hearts furnished words that our lips gladly sung,
    To welcome thee, Prince of the Ocean!
And some, as they looked on thee, thought of their Queen,
As Memory traversed the distance between,
And spoke of the Past—of the years that had been,
    Ere their lives had been link'd to Australia!

Prince Alfred !—whose love for the sons of her land
Hath won a young nation's affection !
Whose undoubting trust, and whose generous hand,
Should have been, in themselves, thy protection ;
We knew how with love, in the far distant sea,
The heart of Britannia was beating for thee ;
But we knew that no kindred were truer than we
Of the bright sunny clime of Australia !

There is grief in our souls that a traitorous foe
Should have slept in the arms of our city ;

There is joy in our innermost hearts that we
    know
Our God hath looked down in His pity!
We shudder to think of the treacherous hand
Whose deed hath wrought shame on an inno-
    cent land—
For the waves never beat on a guardian
    strand
    More loyal than that of Australia!

But ring forth your music, ye merry-toned
    bells,
And tell to the nations our gladness—
That He, who the sands of our lives surely
    tells,
    Hath changed to thanksgiving our sadness!
How the Angel of Mercy hath stooped from
    above.

And sheltered his form with her bright wings
  of love,
That the heart of a trusting Prince surely
  might prove
    He ne'er trusted in vain in Australia!

Coming down the River.

Coming down the river—when the wild-faced night is creeping o'er—
When the wayward ripples chime like distant bells along the shore;
Where the matted trees are fondly bending o'er the waterside,
And the dripping oars are faintly flashing in the gurgling tide!
O, the shadows glance, and the green leaves dance,

Where the dying day-beams quiver!
And the parting song is borne along—
And the stars above seem bright with love,
As we float adown the river!

Coming—coming down the river—and the
 heart with love is light—
Hark! the merry laughter ringing thro' the
 deep'ning frown of night!
How the gentle love-notes linger, till their
 music fades away—
As the dreamy echoes wander wildly o'er the
 sleeping bay!
And the song keeps time with the wavelet's
 chime,
Where the shining moon-streaks shiver,
O the cheek is light, and the eyes are
 bright,

And the faint refrain of the closing strain
    Comes softly down the river !

Coming—coming down the river—when the
    love-tale has been sung,
And the old folks whisper of the gladsome
    days when they were young !
When the spirit's present pleasure banishes
    each vain regret,
And the eager heart is fraught with scenes
    we never may forget !
    O the dark eyes shine, whilst a hand is in
        mine,
    And I thrill with its magical quiver ;
    And fond words slip from loving lips—
    And the oar in the glassy water dips,
        As we float adown the river !

COMING DOWN THE RIVER.

Coming—coming down the river—when our
    lives are growing old—
When the silvery dross of Age is mingling
    with our curls of gold !
When the dark and sunless waters, with their
    wild and weird-like speech,
Bear us forth to leave us on the Future's
    mist-enshrouded beach !
    May a gentle voice bid my heart rejoice
        That the spirit seeks its Giver !
    May the same sweet song be borne along,
    Till my life shall stray as softly away
        As a ripple that fades from the river !

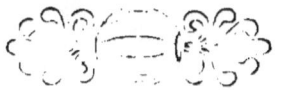

Songs and Ballads.

The Australian Stockman's Song.

THE sun peers o'er the wooded ridge,
    And through the forest dense,
Its golden edge from the mountain ledge
    Looks down on the stockyard fence—
            Looks down,
Looks down on the stockyard fence!
And dark creeks rush thro' the tangled brush,
    Where shuddering shadows throng,
Until they chime with the rude rough rhyme
    Of the wild " goburra's " * song—

---

* *Goburra* is the aboriginal name of the bird commonly known
in Australia as the " Laughing Jackass."

Till they chime—Ha, ha!
Till they chime—Ha, ha!
With the wild " goburra's" song.

The night owl to her home hath fled,
    To shun the glorious pomp
Of the golden day, she speeds away
    To her nest in the tea-tree swamp—
        Away
To her nest in the tea-tree swamp!
The dingo looks with a timid stare,
    As he stealthily prowls along,
And his pattering feet in concert beat
    With the wild " goburra's " song—
        Till they beat—Ha, ha!
        Till they beat—Ha, ha!
With the wild " goburra's " song.

O let them boast their city's wealth,
   Who toil in the dusty town—
Give me the beam on the forest stream,
   And the range's dark-faced frown—
           The stream,
And the range's dark-faced frown !
Where our steeds shall pass o'er the quiver-
   ing grass,
   And the crack of the sounding thong
Shall bid the startled echoes join
   The wild " goburra's " song.
      Till they join—Ha, ha !
      Till they join—Ha, ha !
The wild " goburra's " song.

"There's no such Word as Fail."

THE brightest day may have a cloud
　　Its golden tints to shade—
Fair as it seems, the loveliest flower
　　That earth can yield will fade.
And thus in Life—it matters not
　　How fair the morning dawns,
'Tis clouded o'er—its sweetest flow'r
　　Is garnished still with thorns!
　　　But o'er Life's troubles and its storms,
　　　　If still you would prevail,
　　　Be this your watchword—this your cry—
　　　　There's no such word as fail!"

Think not our lot in Life's decreed
    By fate, or fairy elves—
The joys or sorrows that we bear
    Are fashioned by ourselves!
Should we the burden heavy deem,
    Despair but makes it worse;
'Tis ours to make the future prove
    A blessing—or a curse!
      Then strive!—and surely as the sun
        Returns to light the vale,
      So surely will experience prove
        " There's no such word as fail!"

The very stars that for a time
    Are hidden from the gaze—
As ineffectual as they seem,
    Still pierce the midnight haze!

And, one by one appearing, plant
    Their standards in the skies,
Till the dark dome is studded o'er
    With gems—like angel eyes!
      Thus struggle on, when downward bow'd
        In life's tempestuous gale—
      And soon returning joys will prove
        " There's no such word as fail!"

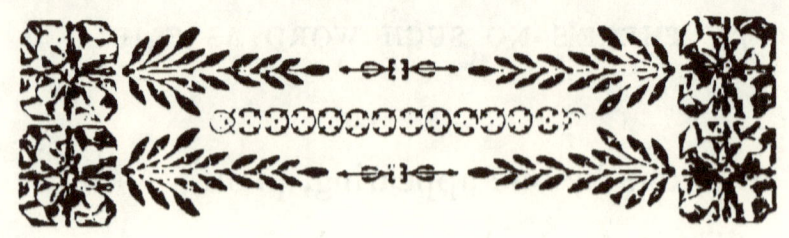

The Cricket on the Hearth.

"Mine has been a happy home, John; and I love the cricket for its sake."—*Charles Dickens.*

The firelight that sparkles in gladness,
    Shines bright on the window and wall;
Peeping out where the trees in their sadness
    Seem wrapped in a funeral pall:
Their spectre-like branches are waving
    Aloft on the storm-ridden air,
And the tempest-winds madly are raving,
    Like the death shrieks of one in despair;
But tho' the storm whistles without, John,
    Exulting in pitiless wrath—

There's a merry voice chirping within, John,
  'Tis the cricket that sings on the hearth!
           Chirp—chirp—chirp!
  'Tis the cricket that sings on the hearth!

When day-gleams o'er mountains are stealing,
  When darkly the night-shadows fall;
Its fairy-like tones, richly pealing,
  Seem breathing a welcome to all:
The old room has echoed above it
  As it carolled in innocent glee.
And O! for its sweet song I love it,
  For it made my home happy to me!
And when I in terror have quail'd, John,
  'Neath the cares that encompassed my path,
There's a voice which to cheer me ne'er fail'd,
  John,

'Tis the cricket that sings on the hearth
Chirp—chirp—chirp
'Tis the cricket that sings on the hearth!

Her Memory lingers yet.

A SWEET song falls upon my heart,
    Like gentle rain on withering leaves—
A song that never may depart
    With every thought enweaves!
It speaks of one whom Time endears,
Of one who still my memory cheers,
    And whispers, " Calm each vain regret,
    For though thine eyes with tears are wet,
Through every chance and change of years
    Her smile will linger yet !"
And thus I treasure, day by day,
    The gentle face I loved so well;

When glances sweet, and music gay,
    Would Fancy's fondest dreams dispel.
But ah! thro' life, my boyhood's queen
    I never, never can forget—
For, like a star at midnight seen,
    Her memory lingers yet!

We loved, as only they can love
    Whose souls like twining buds enwreathe,
When storm or sunshine rests above,
    And flowers or thorns beneath!
No cloud bedimmed Affection's ray,
Though darkness mingled with our day—
    For when by anxious cares beset,
    Love dried the cheek with sorrow wet,
And, like the bow on Ocean's spray,
    It gilded each regret!

And so we loved till envious Death
　　Dissolved the bright enchanting spell;
And, fading 'neath his fatal breath,
　　Alas! my beauteous blossom fell!
Ah me! the long, long years may roll—
　　But still, as when in youth we met,
Unchanged—unfading—in my soul
　　Her memory lingers yet!

Think of me!

THINK of me when twilight shadows
   Gather in the purple west,
When the sunshine has departed,
   And the song-birds seek their nest;
When the wayward winds are whisp'ring
   Over fern and forest tree,
Think that so each eve returning,
   Brings sweet memories, love, of thee!
                Think of me!

Think of me when warring waters
   Roll their restless waves between;

Stand upon the shore, and ponder
    All the joys that might have been ;
Watch the wheeling gull's reflection
    Winging landward from the sea ;
Think, that o'er life's weary ocean,
    So my thoughts fly back to thee !
            Think of me !

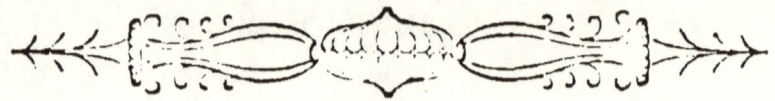

Only of Thee, Love.

Tho' Beauty to lure me her charms may discover,
   And voices fall soft as the song of the sea,
No pleadings of friendship, no smile of a lover,
   Can make my thoughts wander, my dear one, from thee!
For when the bright beams of the morning are breaking,
When gently the dew-laden branches are shaking,
When the glories of day the fair earth are forsaking,

I think then of thee, darling, only of thee!
Only of thee!

Tho' love-glancing eyes may conspire to estrange me,
And fair cheeks with rosier blushes may shine;
No eye is so bright that its beauty can change me,
Or wither a love that's as faithful as mine!
For others, to please thee, a false smile may borrow,
Whose sunshine will fade 'neath the storms of to-morrow,
But, dearest, believe me, in gladness or sorrow,
My thoughts with affection turn only to thee!
Only to thee!

There is not a form in existence so smiling,
  But Sorrow will leave on its beauty a trace;
There is not a planet, the darkness beguiling,
  That ne'er had a cloudlet to shadow its face!
But only of thee, love, when Fortune smiles fairest,
Only of thee when her blessings are rarest,
My heart shall regard thee as nearest and dearest,
  My thoughts shall be ever, and only, of thee!
    Only of thee!

Stars of Heaven.

The stars had lit their peaceful fires,
    And quivered on the wild creek's flow,
The forest breezes tuned their lyres
    And breathed in murmurs, soft and low;
Their gentle music sweetly fell—
    Then swiftly to the stars uprose,
As if some tale of love 'twould tell
    To lull the tremblers to repose!

The envious clouds across the sky
    Their misty curtains quickly drew,

As if their malice to defy,
   The silvery stars still brighter grew!
" And thus it is in life," I cried,
   " Man views with fear the tempest lour;
But 'tis when clouds his fame would hide,
   He shines still brighter than before!"

Beside the Garden Gate.

I LINGER'D near the garden gate
    One balmy summer's eve—
Tho' Night drew on with rapid strides
    I linger'd, loth to leave;
For there beneath the cottage-porch,
    Hung with the clustering vine,
A fair cheek on my bosom leant,
    A hand was lock'd in mine!

I told her we must parted be,
    Perchance for many years;

But still our faith should never fail—
    (She answered with her tears.)
Tho' Ocean's waves might roll between,
    Our love need not abate—
I whisper'd, we should meet again
    Beside the garden gate!

Long years rolled on, and I return'd—
    The place was changed, 'tis true;
Among the forms that gather'd round,
    Full many a face seem'd new;
But there was one—remembered well—
    To welcome me did wait,
With looks, with smiles, with heart unchang'd,
    Beside the garden gate!

Fragments from "Kiandra."

(AN EARLIER POEM.)

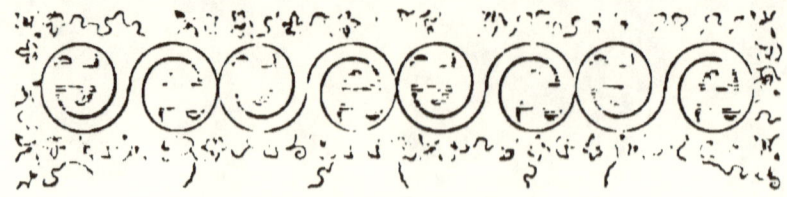

Ninety-five Days Out.

Across the Ocean's heaving breast
    A snow-plumed sea-bird winged its way,
And seemed to brave each briny wave
    That upwards hurl'd the tinted spray,
Where billows—gorgeously arrayed,
    Flung back the golden smile of day.

For as upon the sluggish deep
    The hallowed light of morn did stream,
The waters wakened from their sleep,
    As starts a maiden in her dream,

And through whose half-transparent vest
    The throbbings of the heart are seen!

The sea-breeze, like the breath of love,
    Came sweeping o'er the speckled main,
Now soaring to the skies above,
    Now, creeping o'er the liquid plain,
The wave-born accents lingered like
    The harpings of a solemn strain!

A vessel glided, where the spray
    Around her cast a jewelled screen;
She stole––a bright ethereal fay!
    Adown some fair enchanted scene—
Or towered upon her ocean throne,
    Exalted like a Naiad queen!

Upon her deck two beings stood
    Flushed with the morning's crimson light,
Gazing upon the blue-robed flood
    With pearly sea-gems all bedight!
Then from them turned to a lone sea-bird,
    Winging afar its restless flight.

The one—a man of iron nerve,
    With features proud and sternly cast,
The vivid gleaming of whose eye—
    Tho' brief—spoke strangely of the past,
Like dull fires re-enkindled by
    The breathings of a sudden blast.

And by his side a girlish form—
    Supported by his arm—reclined,
As some frail plant its tendril arm
    Around a rugged oak will bind,

And fondly garb its ancient friend
   Till their green locks are entertwined.

Bright as those forms of loveliness
   Which we in sleep-wrought visions seek,
She—like those transient phantoms shone
   As lovely—yet withal so meek!
While—rippling waves—the golden curls
   Stole softly down her sunny cheek.

Still she was sad—recurring thoughts,
   (That vast, and oft unwelcome crowd!)
Struck on her heart-strings, sorrow fraught,
   And drew forth music, wild and loud;
And a tear upon her lashes hung
   Like light upon a summer cloud.

Tho' for a season, mortal joy
   From care may separated be,
Still—like an isle-divided stream
   United ere it joins the sea—
So, love and hate, so, smiles and tears,
   In human life commingled be!

Wild songs came wafted o'er her soul,
   As memory tuned the sweet refrain;
She strove to check its harpings, but
   Alas! her strivings were in vain:
She sought to burst the fetters—ah!
   'Twas then she felt how strong the chain!

   *   *   *   *   *   *

Darkly loom'd Night's sombre visage,
   Darkly frown'd she on the world,

And her star-emblazoned standard
    O'er the ocean was unfurled!
While the daylight's dying struggle—
    Like the mist dispersed—upcurled.

Softly moaned the sobbing waters
    'Neath Australia's rock-bound shore,
Singing gently, like a love-song,
    Sleeping nature, sailing o'er!
Then amid the wave-worn caverns
Sighing with a solemn roar.

Like some knight of ancient story,
    With a footstep soft as sleep!
Stealing past the frowning portals
    Of a tyrant's donjon keep!
So between the Heads the vessel
    Glided on the sobbing deep!

Glided like a mystic vision—
    O'er the water's surfless breast ;
Then she furled her moonlit pinions
    Like a weary bird at rest :
And the harbour's rippling wavelets
    Sang a welcome to their guest !

Morning in the Australian Alps.

O'er the distant eastern mountains,
Day hath pour'd her golden fountains,
And the landscape dim is dreaming
  Like a picture vaguely drawn ;
Where the sunbeams, swift advancing,
O'er the rugged range are glancing,
And in mellow kisses streaming
  On the blushing cheek of morn !

Slowly comes the sunlight creeping,
Where the night—cold tear-drops weeping—
Lingers like a touch of sorrow
  Over Nature's slumbering form !

Comes—like Hope—Faith's brightest off-
    spring !
Like the tempest-conquering day-spring,
Ushering in a glorious morrow,
    All the brighter for the storm.

Upward speeding—never heeding
Where the vanquish'd night, receding,
Gathers all its scatter'd forces
    In the gullies far below;
Upward springs the morn-beam shining,
Round the misty crag-tops twining,
Leaving, as it onward courses,
    On their peaks a crimson glow.

Bright as dreams which nought embitters,
Even so the sunlight glitters,

On the pendant dewy tear-drop,
   Stealing down the white gum's side;
Quivering like the thought of duty
In the kindling eye of beauty,
Or the trembling costly ear-drop
   On the pale cheek of a bride!

Then, like souls who 've nobly striven,
Soaring to the verge of Heaven,
Down it throws its loving glances
   To the vap'rous plains beneath;
Where the creek's redundant bosom,
Slyly tempts each purple blossom,
Laughing, as it forth advances,
   From the night-fog's fading wreath!

Now among the reeds it gushes,
Now across its rock-bed rushes,

Singing with a joyous pleasure
    In the growing light of day;
Snatching up the blossoms shower'd
From mimosas, golden-flower'd,
Hurrying with the stolen treasure
    Down into the valleys grey!

All is silent save the mellow
Tinkle of the bell-bird—Yellow
Stream the fast increasing day-gleams
    On the verdant sward below;
Now in gorgeous colours sparkling—
Now in sombre shadows darkling—
Evanescent as the day-dreams
    Which in slumber come and go!

On the verdure-mantled mountain,
Shimmering on the gushing fountain,

Forth the red refulgence wanders
On the granite peaks uphurl'd;
Surely skies were never lighter—
Surely earth was never brighter,
When, in all its pristine grandeur,
Day first beam'd upon the world!

Gibbs, Shallard, and Co., Printers, Pitt Street, Sydney.

www.ingramcontent.com/pod-product-compliance
Lightning Source LLC
Chambersburg PA
CBHW020928230426
43666CB00008B/1611